# Horse Facts Book
## For Kids

Copyright©2022HarmonyWells

Horses have been around since about 55 million years ago, although their earliest ancestor was no bigger than a large dog.

Since the time they were first domesticated, about 6,000 years ago, humans have used horses as companions, as working animals, in equestrian sports, and more.

There are over 600 horse breeds in the world today. A genetic study showed that all modern horses come from two ancient horses breeds: the Arabian and Turkoman horses.

Horses can be taught many tasks, as they are very intelligent animals.

They learn quickly, and remember complex tasks. They can also cooperate, and work as part of a team.

Horses are pack animals. They can suffer from loneliness, just as humans do. Horse family groups in the wild usually consist of one or two stallions, several mares, and their foals.

Since horses are prey animals in the wild, when they take time to eat and sleep, one horse will stand guard.

Mares usually just have one baby at a time. The foals will stay with their mothers for up to two years in the wild.

Within a few hours of birth, horses are able to walk and run.

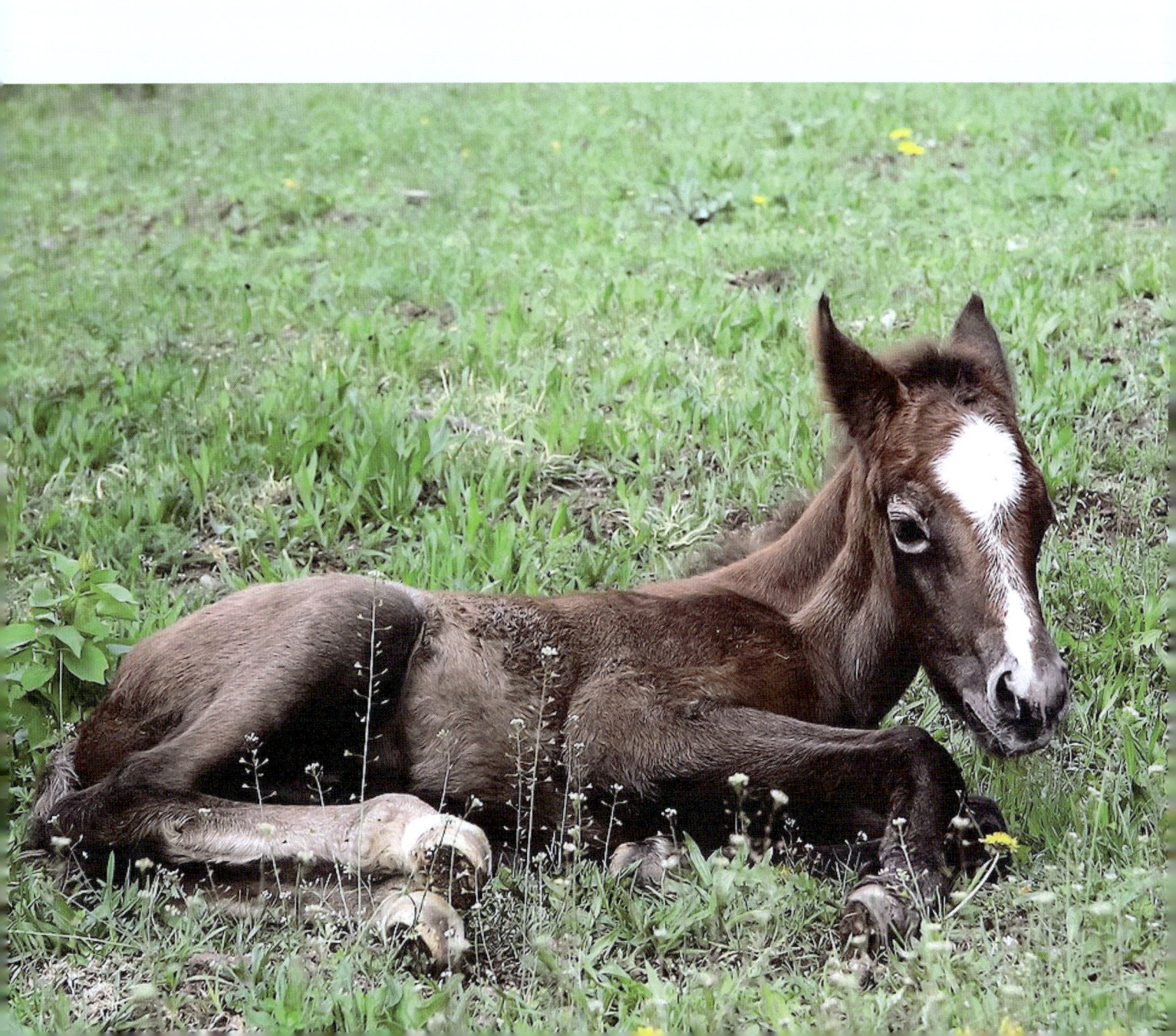

As they get older, colts will break off into bachelor herds. Fillies will stay with their original herd, or start a new herd with a bachelor stallion.

Walk, trot, canter, and gallop are the four natural gaits of most horses.

A normal gallop speed for horses is around 27 mph. The fastest sprinting speed recorded was 55 mph.

Horses have a high social intelligence, and will mourn the passing of a companion.

They form strong social bonds, and can recognize each other and form friendships.

Young horses especially, need to be around other horses, so they can learn the manners and skills that they need to develop. People can only satisfy part of a horse's need for companionship.

They will bray, bite, trample their feet, or grunt to communicate with other horses in their herd.

Horses can recognize a human's mood from their facial expression. They can tell if you're happy or angry. They remember your emotions, and react positively or negatively based on those emotions.

Facial expressions communicate their moods and feelings. They can also show how they are feeling through snorts and whinnies.

According to a study done, snorts mean horses are content. Whinnies in shorter, lower frequencies expressed positive emotions, while higher, more lengthy whinnies indicated negative emotions.

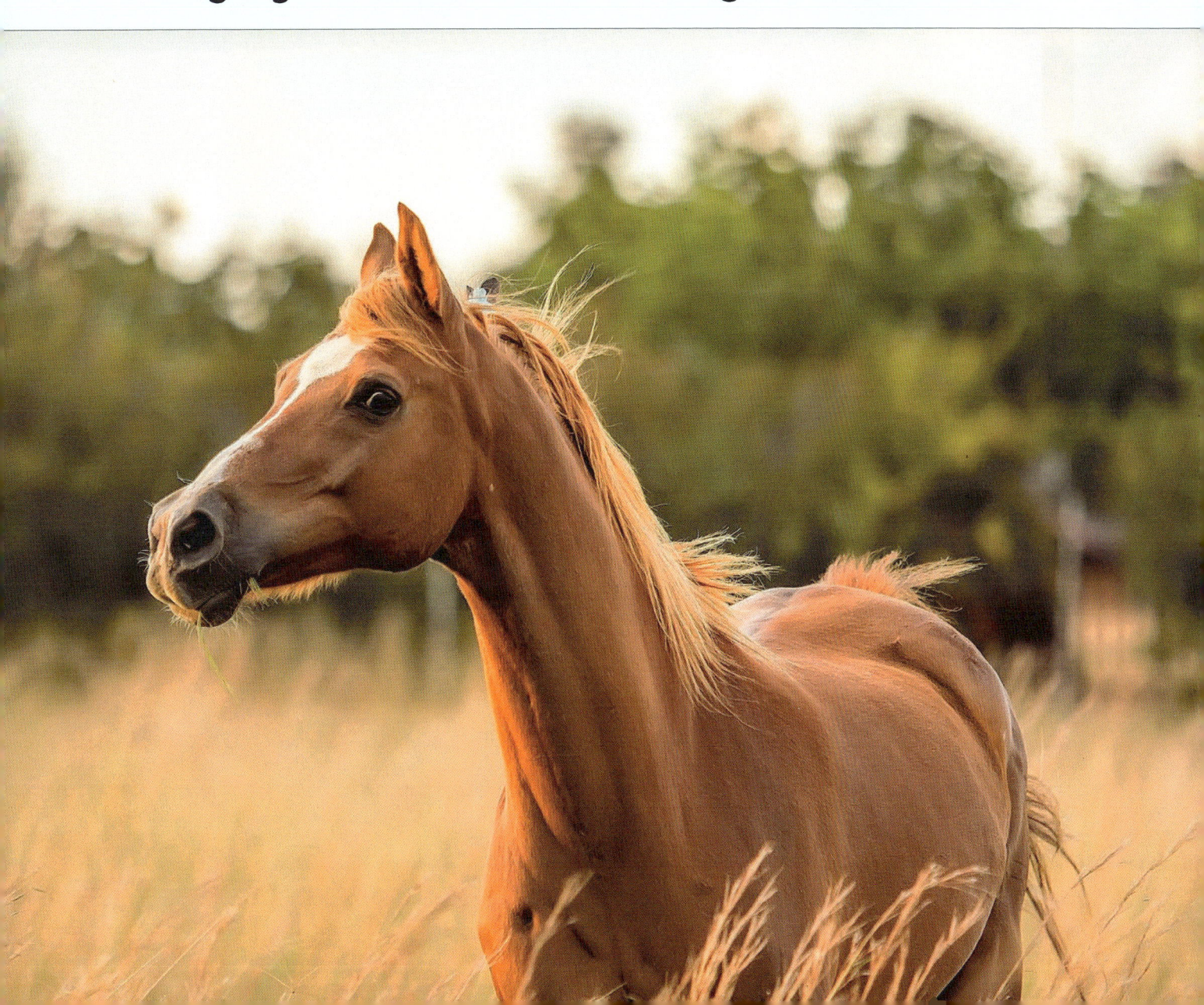

Horses have very fast reflexes, and can deliver a powerful kick in less than one second.

A fixed pelvis limits their lateral motion.

Horses have the biggest eyes of any land mammal.

Because their eyes are positioned on the sides of their head, horses can see nearly 360 degrees. They have only two blind spots, one directly in front of them below their nose, and one directly behind them.

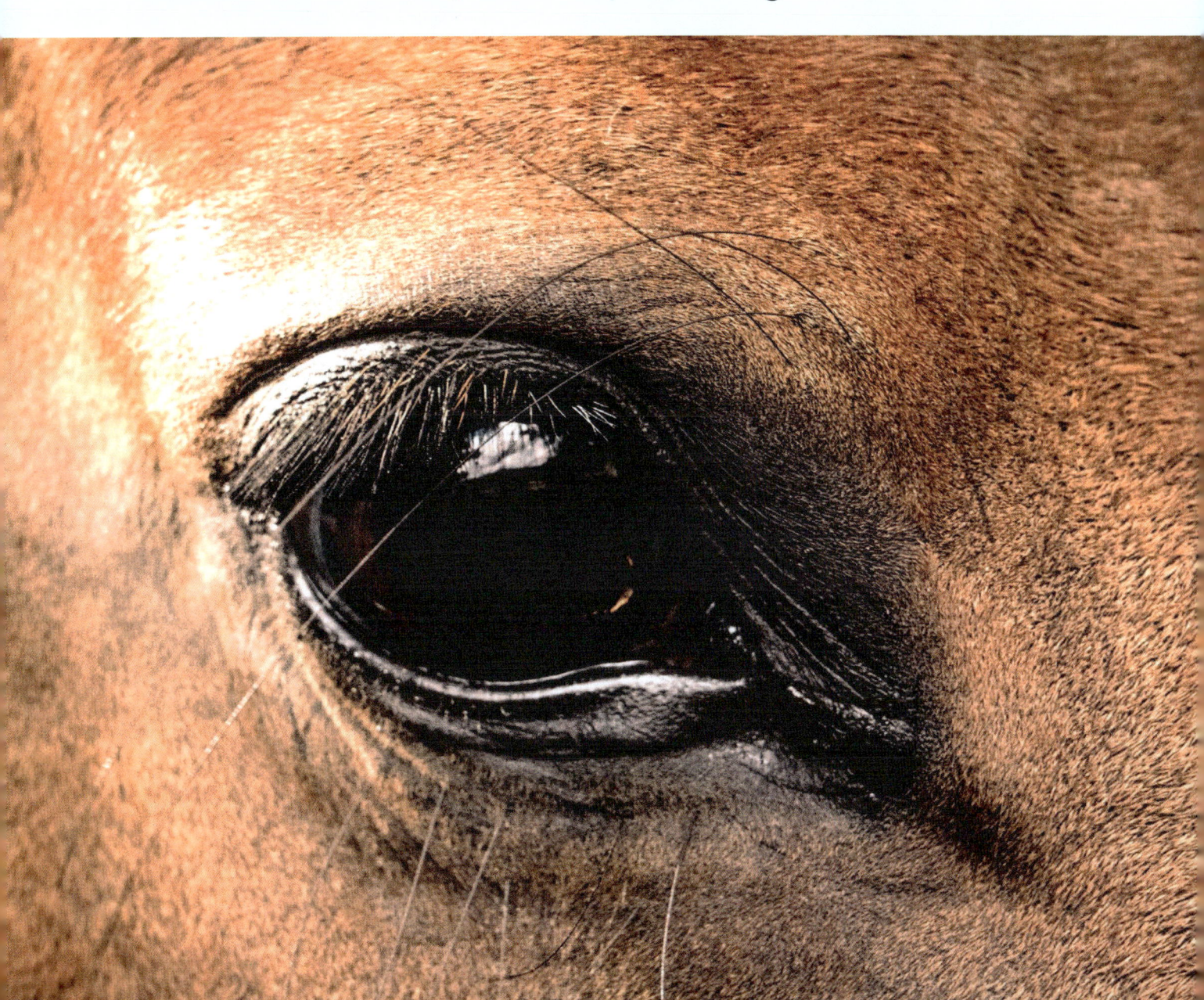

Horses can move their eyes separately, and focus on two different things at one time. Their ears will usually point in the direction where the eye on the same side is looking.

However, most of their vision is monocular, and therefore they have poor depth perception

They also have limited color perception. They can see blue and yellow, but not red. They are red-green colorblind.

Their ears can rotate almost 180 degrees because they have 10 muscles in each ear (humans only have 3). They can also move them independently of each other.

Horses are not able to breathe through their mouth. They can only breathe through their nose.

For a horse's stomach to work efficiently, it needs to always have food in it. That is why they eat for 16-18 hours per day. More than a few hours without food could cause them to develop stomach ulcers.

Their digestive system is strictly a one way path, and they do not have the ability to throw up, or even to burp.

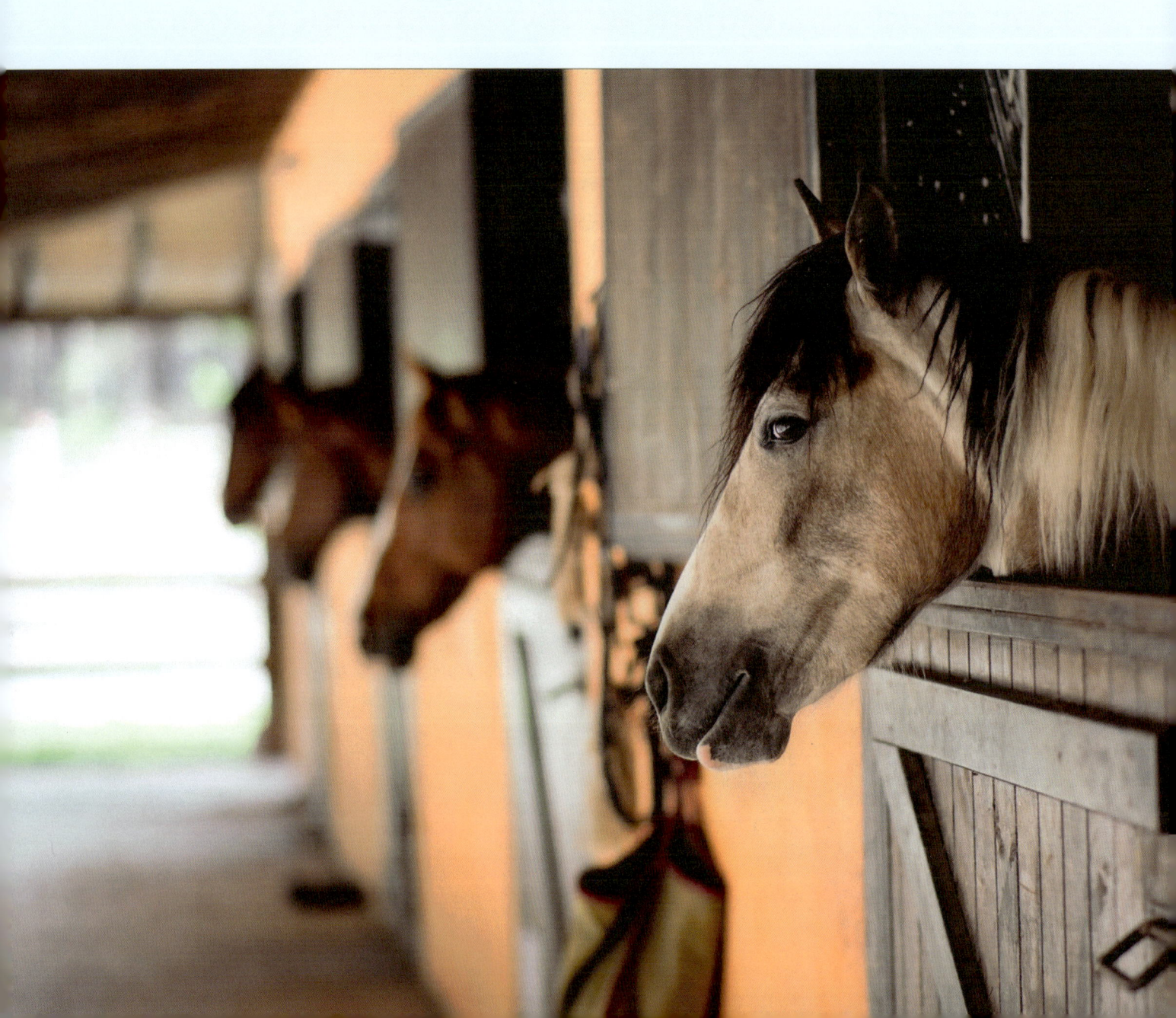

Horse hooves are made from keratin, the same protein that human fingernails are made from.

Horseshoes are used to protect the horse's feet and hooves, and so that the hooves don't wear down too quickly.

When horses lift their upper lip, they're engaging in what's called the flehmen response. It pushes a scent deeper into their nose, so they can determine whether the smell is good or bad.

Horses have a system of ligaments and tendons that allow them to lock their legs, so that they can relax while in a standing position.

Although horses can sleep lightly while standing up, they also need to lie down for short periods of time for a deeper sleep. Lying down for too long puts a lot of pressure on their bones and organs.

Horses drink 5-10 gallons of water daily. They have three pairs of salivary glands, and can produce up to 10 gallons of saliva every day.

Horses may roll on the ground for several reasons, including to scratch an itch, or roll in mud to keep bugs off. It can also mean that they have a buildup of gas in their intestines, which could lead to colic.

Most horses have 205 bones, with a few exceptions, such as the Arabian, which only has 201 bones.

Because they are smart, horses get bored easily, and can develop bad habits if they are in a stall for long hours. They like to play and run around.

The oldest horse ever, Old Billy, lived 62 years. The average lifespan of a horse is 25-30 years.

The world's smallest horse ever was a dwarf miniature horse named Thumbelina. She was just 17.5 inches tall, and weighed just 57 pounds.

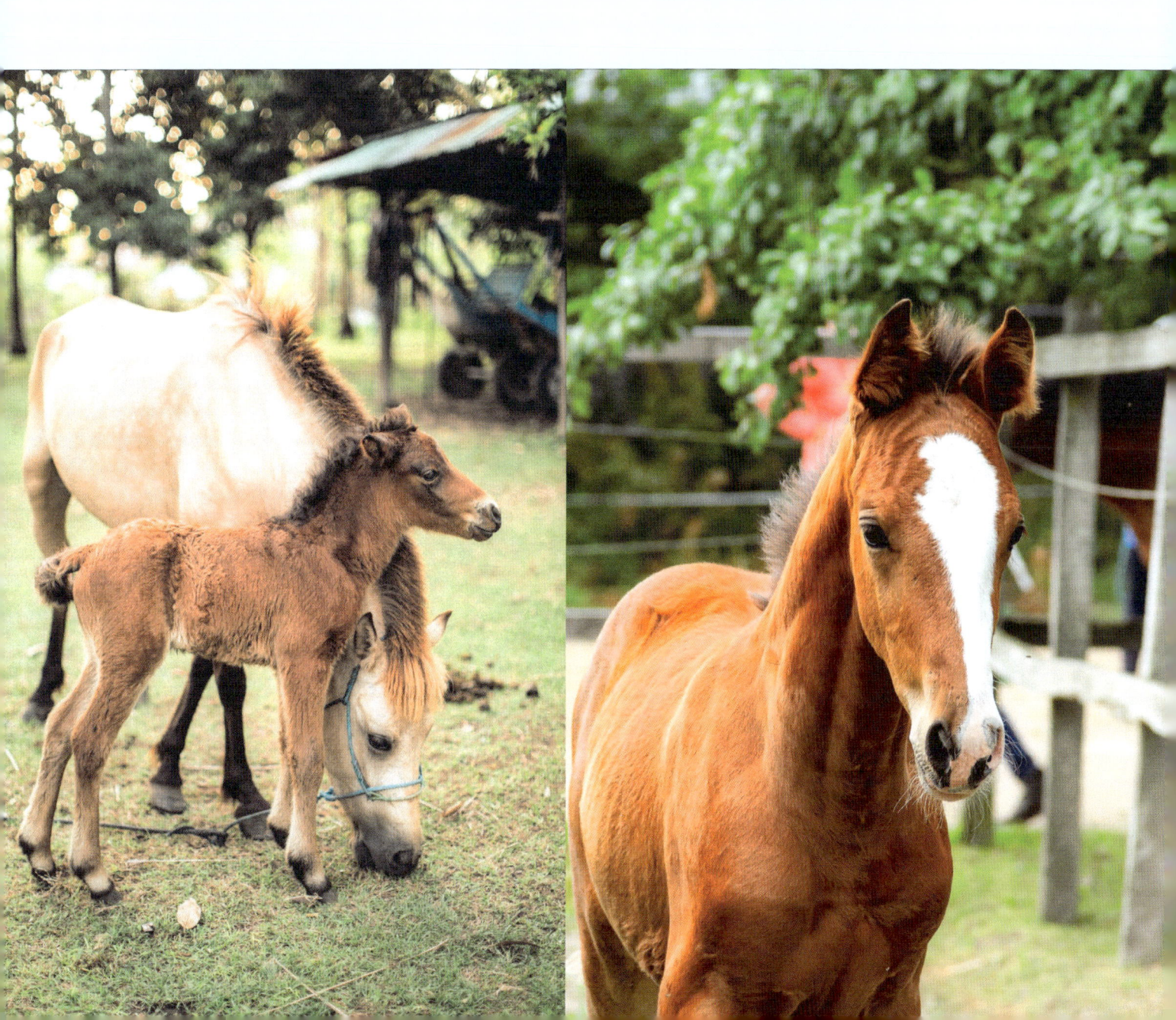

The biggest horse ever was called Sampson, and he was over seven feet tall at the withers (base of the neck, above the shoulders). He weighed 3,360 pounds.

The highest measured jump by a horse was 8 feet 1.25 inches.

There are no longer any true "wild" horses. The horses that roam freely are descendants of domestic horses that escaped.

Equine-assisted therapy and hippotherapy can be helpful for people with many kinds of disorders and diseases, including Down syndrome, autism, and cerebral palsy.

Today horses are found on every continent except Antarctica. The United States has more horses than any other country.

# Bonus Facts

Males have more teeth than females.

The most expensive horse ever sold was a Thoroughbred racehorse called Fusaichi Pegasus, which sold for $70 million.

The most popular breeds are the American Quarter Horse, the Thoroughbred and the Arabian.

The rarest horse breed is the Sorraia, with fewer than 200 left.

Donkeys, zebras, and rhinos are their closest relatives.  All of these animals have an odd number of toes.

The Gypsy Vanner horse breed grow mustaches.

# **Bonus Facts**

Most horses weigh about 1,000 pounds.

Horses don't have collarbones.

In 10-12 months they can regrow an entire hoof.

A horse's heart can weigh up to 9 or 10 pounds, and is over 10 times bigger than human hearts.

Twin horses are possible, but are extremely rare.

Albino horses do not exist.

Horses can smell fear, and happiness, through the body odors that humans emit.

Printed in Great Britain
by Amazon